The weather is always changing.

Day and night and year-round, forecasters at
the National Weather Service are busy....

WEATHER FORECASTING

BY GAIL GIBBONS

Aladdin Paperbacks

For Vera Milz

Special thanks to John Machowski, George Adamson, Ray Bliven, Bill Grady, David James, George Joseph, and Joe Luisi of the National Weather Service.

Aladdin Paperbacks. An imprint of Simon & Schuster Children's Publishing Division, 1230 Avenue of the Americas, New York, NY 10020. Copyright © 1987 by Gail Gibbons. All rights reserved including the right of reproduction in whole or in part in any form. Also available in a hardcover edition from Simon & Schuster Books for Young Readers. First American edition. Printed in Hong Kong by South China Printing Company (1988) Ltd.   10   9   8   7   6   5
The text of this book is set in 14 pt. Egyptian 505 Light.
The illustrations are rendered in watercolor with pen and color-tint overlays, and reproduced in full color.
LIBRARY OF CONGRESS CATALOGING-IN-PUBLICATION DATA   Gibbons, Gail. Weather forecasting.
Summary: Describes forecasters at work in a weather station as they use sophisticated equipment to track and gauge the constant changes in the weather.   1. Weather forecasting – Juvenile literature. [1. Meteorological stations. 2. Weather forecasting] I. Title.   QC995.43.G53   1987   551.6   86-7602   ISBN 0-689-71683-4

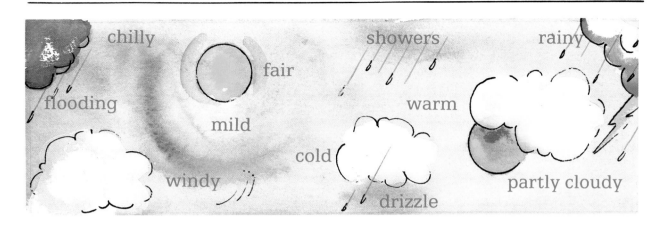

chilly

showers

rainy

fair

flooding

warm

mild

cold

partly cloudy

windy

drizzle

SPRING...

and the weather changes.

Today there are heavy black clouds and it is chilly. It begins to sprinkle rain. Umbrellas are opening.

During the day at the weather station, two weather forecasters and a meteorologist are on duty. At night there is one forecaster. Weather conditions are updated around the clock.

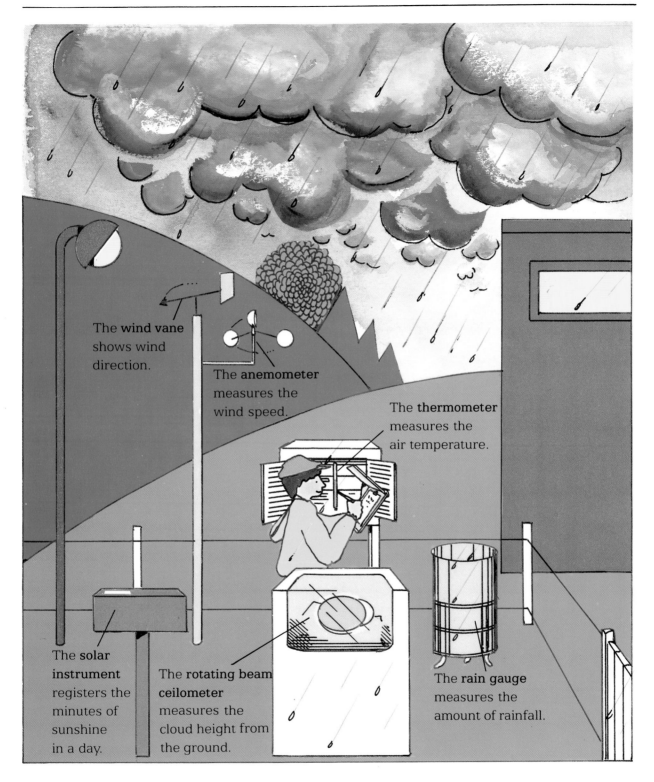

The **wind vane** shows wind direction.

The **anemometer** measures the wind speed.

The **thermometer** measures the air temperature.

The **solar instrument** registers the minutes of sunshine in a day.

The **rotating beam ceilometer** measures the cloud height from the ground.

The **rain gauge** measures the amount of rainfall.

Now it's raining. One of the forecasters has gone outside. He takes readings of the instruments and checks sky conditions and visibility. He does this once every hour.

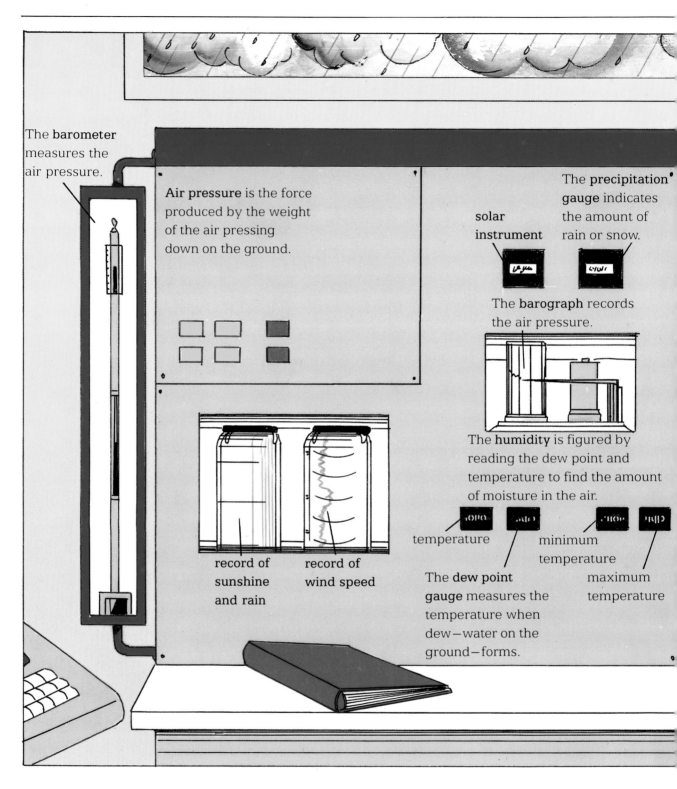

The **barometer** measures the air pressure.

Air pressure is the force produced by the weight of the air pressing down on the ground.

solar instrument

The **precipitation** gauge indicates the amount of rain or snow.

The **barograph** records the air pressure.

The **humidity** is figured by reading the dew point and temperature to find the amount of moisture in the air.

temperature

minimum temperature

maximum temperature

The **dew point** gauge measures the temperature when dew—water on the ground—forms.

record of sunshine and rain

record of wind speed

Back in the station he checks the readings on the observation console. Some of the gauges are connected to some of the outside instruments. They cross-check figures he has already gathered.

This forecaster is interested in what the weather is at the moment. He is called the immediate weather forecaster.

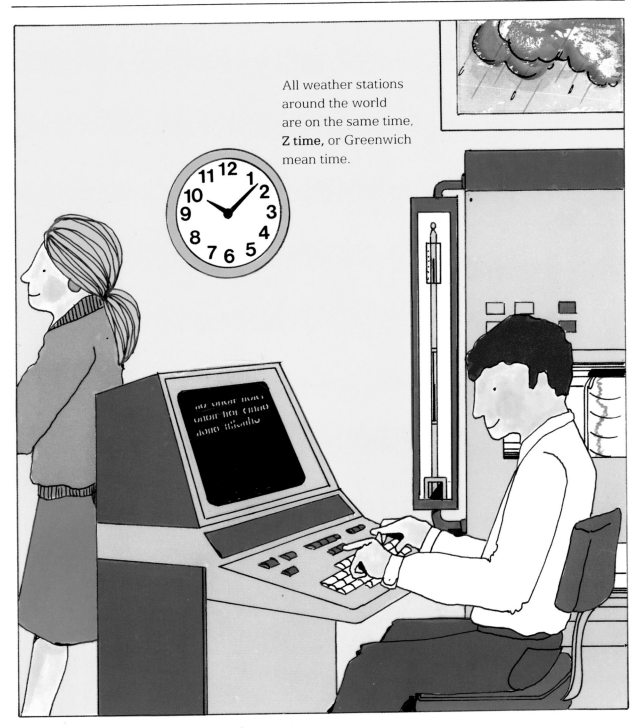

All weather stations around the world are on the same time, **Z time,** or Greenwich mean time.

There are thousands of weather stations and each one reports to the nearest central weather office. When the immediate weather forecaster has all of the hourly statistics, he sends them by computer to his central office. Now weather stations around the world can use the information.

The weather station has a broadcasting system. Every hour, the immediate weather forecaster records his information on tape and slides the tape into a slot. The tape runs continuously as a weather update to weather radio receivers and to radio and television stations. A recording is also made for people who call the National Weather Service for information.

A **weather map** is transmitted from the central weather office.

High pressure is when the air pressure rises. It is usually cold and dry air.

Low pressure is when the air pressure falls. It is usually hot and moist air.

A **satellite weather map** is a picture of the weather patterns from a satellite.

The **weather radar monitor** shows precipitation.

The other weather forecaster is concerned with the long-range, or extended, forecast. She gathers information to predict the weather for tonight, tomorrow, and the following day. A storm area appears on the screens. That means it will rain locally for quite some time. A high-pressure system is about one day away. This will bring cooler weather and sunshine.

The forecaster checks with the central weather office to see if its predictions match hers. Now she writes her extended forecast and types it into the computer. She does this every six hours so that other weather stations will have an up-to-date extended forecast for the area. She also records the forecast for broadcasting.

A **tornado** is a destructive funnel-shaped cloud.

Information comes in on the computer. A tornado has touched down in the midwest. There is some damage. Locally it continues to rain hard. The immediate weather forecaster goes outside to take the hourly readings.

SUMMER ...

and the weather changes.

Today almost everyone is at the beach. It is very hot and sunny.

cumulus clouds

Outside the weather station the hourly readings are taken. Visibility is clear and the clouds are white and puffy in the sky. They are cumulus, or fair-weather, clouds.

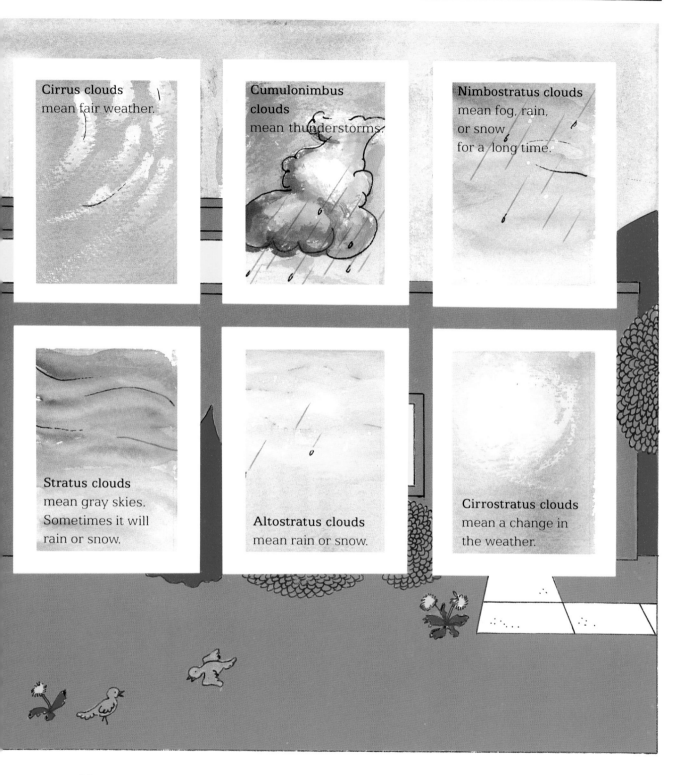

Cirrus clouds mean fair weather.

Cumulonimbus clouds mean thunderstorms.

Nimbostratus clouds mean fog, rain, or snow for a long time.

Stratus clouds mean gray skies. Sometimes it will rain or snow.

Altostratus clouds mean rain or snow.

Cirrostratus clouds mean a change in the weather.

Clouds are weather indicators. The weather forecasters study them all the time.

An **air mass** is a body of air with the same temperature and moisture.

A **front** is a line of changing weather between two kinds of air masses.

One of the forecasters and the meteorologist watch the weather map. A cold front is moving into the area. It will push away the hot air. Along the cold front are thunderstorms.

Again the immediate weather forecast is put together. It is read into the microphone. Then the extended forecast is taped.

A call comes in. A pilot wants to know what the weather conditions will be like during his flight tomorrow.

FALL...

and the weather changes.

Leaves blow in the wind. Smoke curls from chimneys. Everyone is dressed in warm clothes.

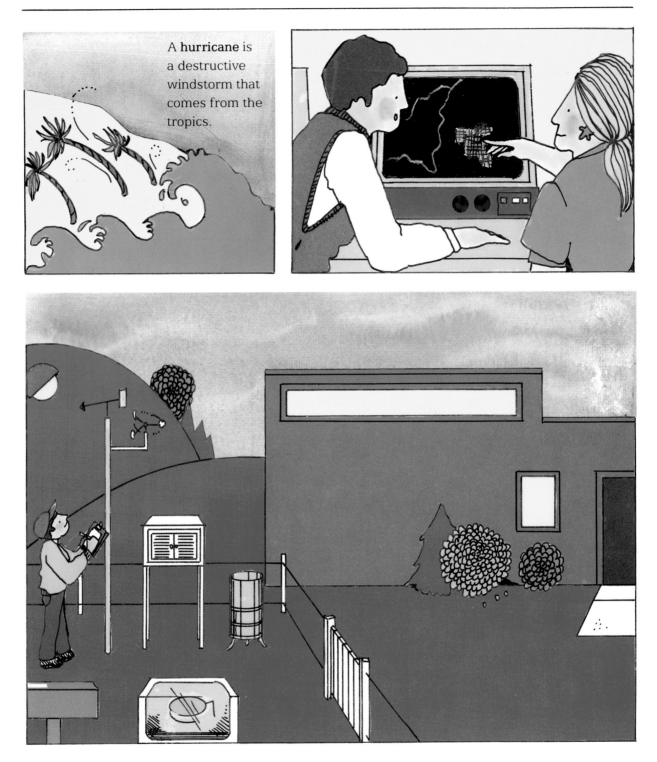

A **hurricane** is a destructive windstorm that comes from the tropics.

The weather forecasters watch the radar monitor. To the south, a hurricane is building in strength. It's moving to the north, toward their area. They constantly check its position. At the same time they update their local weather conditions.

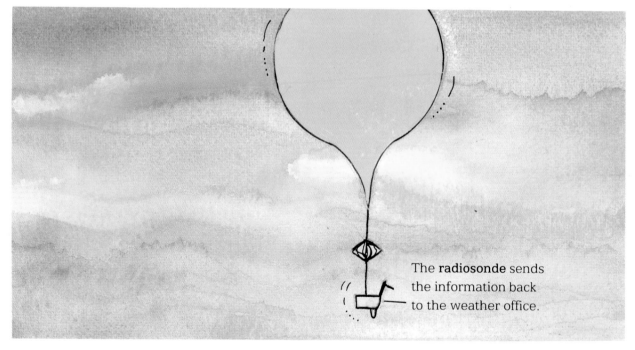

The **radiosonde** sends the information back to the weather office.

Over at the central weather office a weather balloon is released. Certain weather offices are assigned to do this twice a day. As the balloon climbs higher, it signals back to the office changes in temperature, air pressure, and humidity. The information will be available on computer to all weather stations.

Hours later, the forecasters broadcast that the hurricane has changed direction and is going out to sea. If it had stayed on course, they would have broadcast hurricane warnings.

The updates are done again. Low, dark clouds hurry by. Instruments are read and information is checked on the computers. The updated forecasts are put together.

It looks like mild and sunny weather for the next two days. A high-pressure system will move into the area. It will push away the damp and windy weather.

foggy   windy   cold   mild   chilly

cloudy   partly cloudy

blizzard   sunny   snowy

dry   sleet

flurries   hail   partly sunny

WINTER...

and the weather changes.

Today the weather began with blue skies and sun...but now it is snowing hard. It is the first snowstorm of the season.

Storm warnings are broadcast. The snow is drifting and visibility is poor. Very few planes are flying in and out of the airport. Some highways are closed. Snowplows are out at work.

The radar monitor shows that the storm will last through the night. The low-pressure system has brought heavy, wet snow with mild temperatures. The forecasters study the monitor. Six inches of snow and still falling!

Because of the broadcasts that predicted the snowstorm, many people are prepared. Most stay indoors. Businesses close early so workers can get home. Everyone waits for the storm to clear.

Back at the weather station more information is gathered. The snow should taper off in the early morning. A high-pressure system will push it away. Weather information is broadcast again.

The weather is always changing. . . .